# DEDICATION

This book is humbly dedicated to 'The Seekers', those amongst you who are looking for a path and those of you who might be lucky enough to have found it.

**Thanks.**

Thanks go to the family of the Rev. Robert Stephen Hawker for the reproducing of his poem on 'Nectan's Glen'.

Also to the Custodian and staff of the 'Kieve' who ensure the site survives.

Last but not least to Mr Guy Mills by whose belief in a sacred waterfall and the saint who lived there made the 'Kieve' what it is today and also made this book possible.

# Contents

# FOREWORD

*By the Rev. Lionel Fanthorpe.*

It is a great honour and a very real pleasure to be invited to write this foreword.

Professor Rotherham's outstanding historical work here combines the best in objective scholarship and erudition with am open and sensitive approach to the mystery and mythology that surround St. Nectan's Glen. The information provided here enables the visitor to make the most of this truly delightful place.

The derivation of the name "Nectan" involves not only the celebrated Christian saint, but refers back a further millennium to Nechtan, a benign water god from pagan times. In his far off days, there were said to be nine hazel trees-the traditional source of wisdom-growing around St. Nectan's well.

In addition to this gift of wisdom that is said to be bestowed on visitors to the Glen, there is a further gift of healing from the allegedly magical waters.

In addition to its fascinating history and the myths and legends that surround the Glen, it is also an area of outstanding natural beauty, with an atmosphere that can only summed up with an ancient Greek word which , in English, would describe it as "A combination of the beautiful and the good".

**Lionel Fanthorpe.**

(Lionel Fanthorpe is not only a Church of England priest and internationally respected television presenter but, together with his wife Patricia, is an author of many books dealing with the world of the sacred and profane.)

# Introduction

There can be few people, outside of Britain's 'West Country', that will have ever heard of Saint Nectan and the falls that bear his name lying as they do on the outskirts of Tintagel in the beautiful county of Cornwall.

Yet this little known man from the period of history we call today the 'Dark Ages' exudes the same attraction for so many that the site of his hermitage and cell of retreat draw people from all over the country and, indeed increasingly, the world to experience the closeness to the saint and the waterfalls and pool deemed by many to hold the epithet 'sacred' as a place of pilgrimage and reflection. Few sacred sites hold the same draw to both Christian and pagan seekers as Saint Nectan's Glen.

However, why should it be so? As I have mentioned the man himself could never have been classed among the 'A' list of saints in the register! What could it be that brings increasing visitors each year to visit this remote, but exceptionally beautiful site? (It is said the Charles Dickens, that writer of Victorian conscience and virtue, was a visitor to the place and that it also drew no less a person than the great Queen Victoria herself , Empress of India and ruler of the largest empire the world has ever seen was also amongst the list of visitors).

The answer lies, perhaps, in what the 'Falls' actually are and, indeed, what they have symbolized spiritually for so many over the centuries.

This book has been dedicated to the 'Seekers', those amongst us who travel and search for that elusive and indefinable something that affects our spirituality and I like to think that, just maybe, Saint Nectan beat us all to it, found it and subsequently left it for us who follow on to recognize and enjoy in both the esoteric and aesthetic paths we may choose to take.

I trust, dear 'Seeker', that this book will help in some small way to illumine your path as you take on your quest.

St. Nectan

# The Legend

## Saint Nectan. (c.AD 468-510)

e are told that Nectan was from a large and exceptionally fruitful family and one of the many children of King Brychan of Brycheiniog in Wales.

However, we shall be looking at his 'prolific' family in another chapter, here we will deal with the story of the man himself.

The name 'Nectan' is of ancient 'British' descent and here it is well to remember that we are most definitely dealing with Britain and not 'England' as we are talking of the days when the might of Rome has just evacuated the country and the Saxons have yet to gain control over the realm.

Indeed, Nectan is an early form of the name that in more modern times we shall call 'Nathan' and in old Welsh is known as 'Nudd' (pronounced Nith), while the Latin version of his name is Natanus. It's quite possible that Nectan would have been versed in Latin but by no means should we take this for granted, for we are dealing with the country when the old Celtic Christianity was the religion of choice for those that followed the new faith.

It would not be for a peri0od of some years before the 'Roman' church would gain it's hold over Britain and with it the adoption of the rites we have come to know as 'Catholic'. If we are to believe much of that which has been passed down to us the early Celtic church worked quite happily and freely, in the rural areas particularly, with the local inhabitants and their earlier faith and customs. Tolerance and guidance was their message as opposed to domination by force. That is not to say that they themselves were pagan but it may be true to believe that if they could practice their new religion hand in hand with the old faiths then there was little or no reason to obliterate one for the other.

Into this culture then came our Saint Nectan. He is said to have sailed into the West Country by taking a small vessel from South Wales and landing on the border lands of Cornwall and Devon at a place called 'Hartland Point' and, continuing his journey on foot, he came across a valley of some beauty at a location we now call 'Stoke St Nectan' nearby to Hartland.

Running through this valley was an abundant spring of clear and pure water and it is in this vicinity that he built his first church and 'cell' or dwelling place in which he settled it is said for many years.

St. Nectans Waterfall

However, it is near Tintagel in Cornwall, where he built his retreat and where his memory is now kept alive in the name of Saint Nectan's Kieve (actually 'Kieve' means tub and this is certainly due to the effect of the waterfall having created a luxuriously deep pool under the onslaught of its gushing torrent over the centuries).

The most well repeated part of the legend of Nectan is of course the story of the two cows. According to belief it was in the year 510, when Nectan was 42 years old, that a certain swineherd by the name of 'Huddon' arrived in the vicinity of Nectan's cell. He had been sent, as the legend tells us, by his liege lord to track down some breeding sows that had managed to escape from their enclosure. Huddon approached Nectan and asked if he had seen anything of these pigs and whereas Nectan hadn't he agreed to help said swineherd in the pursuit of the errant porkers.

After a long search they managed to locate the escaped bacon and they were duly returned, via Huddon, to the safe custody of the lord who, in his gratitude, presented to Nectan two fine milk cows. Certainly an extravagant 'thanks' for the return of the pigs!

Shortly afterward, on June 17th to be exact, Nectan was out while his cows remained in their byre when two opportunist robbers happened upon the scene. Seeing two unguarded cows they promptly made off with them and, upon his return, Nectan found his animal pen 'sans' cattle!

Going off in pursuit of the villains Nectan eventually came across the perpetrators of the theft and faced them with their misdemeanour. Now, being a holy man he did not approach them with cudgel flailing and beleaguer them around the head for the return of his beasts, no, he preached to them.

Now please bear in mind that we are dealing with two ruffians from the 'Dark Ages' here and I think it is fair to say that they would not be counted amongst the regular congregation at the local church. They decided to shorten his discourse and promptly cut his head off!

So now we have on the scene two villains who have very recently become murderers, two on-looking cows and one holy man minus his head. Picture if you will the look of mild surprise therefore when the said decapitated hermit stands up, retrieves his head and carries it off back to his cell!

We are led to believe that of the two ruffians one died and one went blind.

What happened to the cows is anybodies guess but Nectan makes it safely back, (well as safely back as you could whilst carrying your own head under your arm)

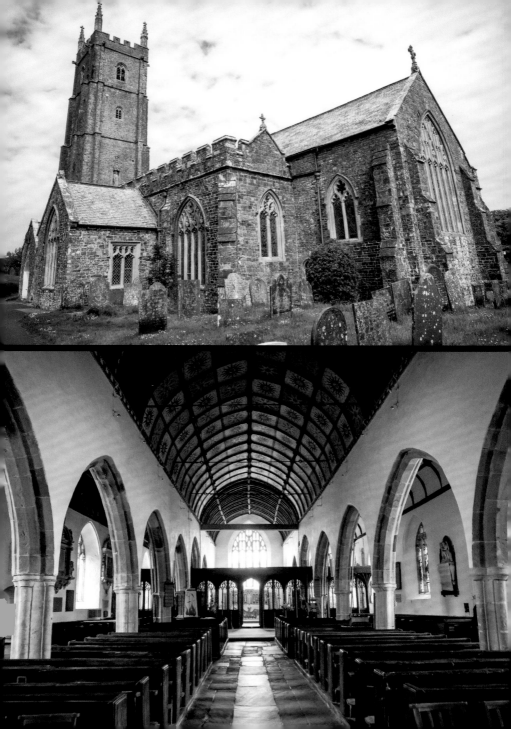

*Page left, page right - St. Nectans Church*

before eventually dying, and certainly at Stoke St Nectan in Devon they believe that there are smears of his blood around his holy well and also, they say, wherever his blood fell foxgloves grew and bloomed, foxgloves were taken by his pilgrims to his shrines when they would make journeys to venerate the saint.

This practice went on well into and after the 'Reformation' of the 16th century.

June 17th has become Nectan's feast day, or day of his remembrance in the church, due to his untimely death on this day at the hands of the two thieves.

An interesting variance on this is down to the fact that in ancient Irish folklore Nectan is actually a water deity where he is listed as a guardian of a sacred well. According to the legend no-one could approach the well but Nectan himself or his 'cup bearers' and should anyone dare to do so and hazard a look into the well they would be immediately struck blind. Strange then, that at Stoke St Nectan, over his sacred well is a stone built arch which houses a pair of large oak doors padlocked against prying eyes.

The whole concept of sacred wells/fountains/pools and waterfalls associated with holy beheadings is by no means unique but we will look at a selection of these in another chapter.

To return to Cornwall and our own Nectan's Kieve we have yet another version of his life and death.

We are informed that Nectan actually came to Cornwall in the year 500 AD and settled in the spot now sacred to him. His fame was such indeed that

legend tells us that the knights of the fabled King Arthur used to visit Nectan at this cell and would spend the night in sacred vigil before receiving his blessing prior to their going on a quest.

Next to his cell he built a chapel and on it was said to have been a tall tower that could be seen for many miles around. In this tower Nectan was said to have placed a small silver bell. When storms threatened the nearby coastline, as only storms can in Cornwall, he was said to climb his tower and ring the bell in an effort to warn any fishermen and shipping who might be out in such weather before it became too bad for them. We have to ask however how much use a small silver bell would be given the fact that Nectan is attempting to warn sailors et al off the coastline some distance away! Never the less, we are told that during stormy weather the bell can still be heard in its desire to assist seafaring folk to this day. It is also said that only the true believer can hear it as Nectan wanted it to ring true for the followers of the Celtic Christian faith at a time when the Roman church was attempting to make its mark in Britain.

Having lived a fruitful life, we are told that Nectan passed away at the age of 42 years. Now this might seem an early death to us but not so the case in the early 6th century. Legend tells us that two of his many sisters came to attend to him, in fact we are told that of his many siblings a large amount of them went into the church, helped him evangelize the West Country and would gather at Nectan's home each New Year (Or Christmas depending on the version you read), and after his passing he was laid in a coffin of a hollowed oak tree trunk, (this was a common form of burialpractice for someone of standing at this point in history) and that they then diverted the course of the river that flowed at his cell and buried him in the river bed at an undisclosed spot before setting the river back on its true course thus concealing his resting place forever. The two sisters remained at Nectan's cell by his 'Falls' and stayed many years. Local legend states that the local folk were suspicious of them and one day as some of the locals came close to the chapel of the cell they found one of the sisters dead and the other kneeling over her in prayer. She knelt quite still and the folk were able to bury the sister but upon their return they found the other sister still kneeling, she had in fact also died in the company of her sister and their bodies were buried together. Yet another version of this story is associated with the well and sisters of St Nighton but of course the truth may be hidden for eternity, (along with the ever present stories of 'buried treasure' and thesearch for the silver bell)!

A very pleasant poem was penned by the Rev. Robert Stephen Hawker to commemorate the story and I have pleasure including it here:

St. Nectans Chapel

THE PARISH OF S WINNOW
CHAPEL of SAINT NECTAN, MARTYR

WARNING

*"The Sisters of Glen Nectan".*
*It is from Nectan's mossy steep*
*The foamy waters flash and leap;*
*It is where shrinking wild-flowers grow*
*They lave the nymph that dwells below.*
*But wherefore in this far-off dell*
*The reliques of a human cell,*
*Where the sad stream and lonely wind*
*Bring man no tidings of his kind.*

*"Long years agone," the old man said,-*
*'Twas told him by his grandsire dead,-*
*"One day two ancient sisters came;*
*None there could tell their race or name.*

*"Their speech was not in Cornish phrase.*
*Their garb had signs of loftier days;*
*Slight food they took from hands of men,*
*They withered slowly in that glen.*

*One died,- the others shrunken eye'*
*Gushed till the fount of tears was dry;*
*A wild and withering thought had she,*
*'I shall have none to weep for me.'*

*"They found her silent in the last.*
*Bent in the shape wherein she passed,*
*Where her lone seat long used to stand,*
*Her head upon her shrivelled hand."*

*Did fancy give this legend birth,-*
*The grandame's tale for winter hearth?*
*Or some dead bard, by Nectan's stream,*
*People these banks with such a dream?*

*We know not; but it suits the scene*
*To think such wild things here have been:*
*What spot more meet could grief or sin*
*Choose, at the last, to wither in?*

An interesting point is that a little further down the river from the 'Falls' there are carved into the rocks two small carvings showing what have become known as 'Cretan' mazes. They are believed to be approximately 4,000 years old and are virtually identical to the maze that is inscribed into the hillside at Glastonbury on the famous 'Tor' and might be a spiritual map of the course needed to ascend the maze in order achieve the 'God-head' during ritual.

So there we have the legend and always remember that the difference between legend and myth is that legend has a basis in fact!

**To summarize then:**

During the Dark Ages there was a man called Nectan. *Fact.*

The remains of a 'Hermitage' or cell exist at the site. *Fact.*

Nectan is listed as a great evangelizer of the West Country. *Fact.*

The 'Falls' at the Kieve are known as a sacred site. *Fact.*

He was one of King Brychans many children. *Probability.*

His body lies buried at the 'Kieve'. *Possibility.*

His two sisters mourned and buried his body. *Legend.*

St. Nectans Waterfall

Brychan

# The Family Of Nectan

When dealing with the family background of our saint we must bear in mind that the primary source material, or period documentation, is virtually non-existent. Most of our sources were written many years after the events and this must be remembered when we conduct our studies. Most of what we know stems from the ancient 'Genealogies' of the Welsh, Cornish and Breton people but most were of a later date than the years we are looking at now.

According to the legends and oral traditions Brychan was born in Ireland in 410 AD with his father being King Anlach and his mother Queen Marth or Marchel, also identified as Marchell Tewdrig, a progenitor of the Tudor family, but she herself was of ancient Welsh descent and her family were the rulers of the kingdom of Garthmadrun of which she was heiress.

Interestingly the name Brychan we believe in the ancient tongue, 'brochan' means 'freckled' and this might have been his facial condition and thus his name derived from that. It might even give us a clue as to his appearance as if he was so freckled as to warrant his name being issued from this it might be fair to assume he is of red or 'ginger' haired persuasion. Another point of interest in the orthography of his name is that if you buy a pair of 'brogue' shoes, that are decorated with the punched 'freckling in the leather, the name comes from the old Scots word 'broghan', meaning again the pattern in the leather.

Shortly after the birth of Brychan the family moved to Wales in order that Marth could take up her position and they lived together at a place called Y Fenni-Fach. It would appear that around the age of four years old young Brychan was sent to be schooled by Saint Drichan who by this time was blind and lived along the river Ysgir.

After he had been studying for some seven years it is said the Drichan asked young Brychan to bring him his favourite spear. Using the spear old Drichan pointed with it to a clearing near where they were sat and out of the wooded area came a wild boar and a stag and when he pointed the spear towards the river the fish began leaping around on its surface. Pointing the spear once again at a nearby tree it was seen that from its branches hung a bees nest which was positively dripping with fresh honey. It was from all of this that old Drichan prophesied that young Brychan would have a prosperous and fruitful future. However, we must remember that at this point Drichan was blind! Perhaps we must accept the possibility of a miracle here in the divining of Brychan's future.

In the neighbouring kingdom of Powys the ruler was yet another Irishman called King Banhandle, it would seem he was something of an opportunist and that the kingdom might have come to him owing to an act of usurpation and not by inheritance or legal means. Trouble brewed between the two Irishmen, (Anlach and Banhandle) and before too long war ensued.

However, Bandandles army was considerably more powerful than that of Anlach and to avoid any more blood shed young Brychan was sent by his father to Banhandle as a hostage.

This might seem appalling to us but please remember that the time of which we are speaking was fifteen hundred years ago and the sense of family and values that hold our society together, (well most of the time) were not in evidence then. If you were a monarch or great chieftain it was common for your children to grow up away from you, when, indeed, if you met again it was not uncommon for the parent and child to be total strangers and given these circumstances there would be no 'blood lost' between the generations.

To come forward in time to the 15th century we have yet another occurrence of this sort of hostage 'trade' being practiced when the young Vlad Tepes, (later to come down to be known in history as Vlad Dracul) was hostaged by his father, the king of Wallachia, to the attacking Turks, only then his father attacked the Turks without a thought of his sons safety at all!

When this occurred Brychan was a young man, certainly in his teens, and we are told that he was actually well received at Banhandle's court and treated quite well. Now Branhandle had a daughter called Banhadlwedd and Brychan fell in love with her. His advances however were not welcomed at all and so in a fit of lust Brychan forced himself upon Banhadlwedd. Hardly the type of action one would expect from a future saint!

A short while afterwards Brychan's father King Anlach died and Brychan was allowed to return to home with a , by then, very pregnant Banhadlwedd.

Brychan was made king in the capital 'Caer Efong' by the host of nobles of his old fathers court and was proclaimed king. After the ceremony we are told that Banhadlwedd gave birth to a boy who was to be named Cynog and Brychan affirmed that he was his son and proclaimed this by giving the boy a golden chaplet, or torc, to wear on his head as first born of the king.

(Cynog was later to be Saint Cynog).

According to the sources he somewhat changed his ways and became a paragon of virtue, so much so that the local populace renamed to kingdom to Brycheiniog in his honour. Today, of course, we know it as Brecknock, or Brekknock, sporting as it does the 'Brecon Beacons' range of hills.

He is said to have married three times during his life and, according to one source, produced twenty four children. Now this would be quite an effort in its own right but in other sources the amount of children ranges from twelve up to sixty! I must assume that this accounts for the three marriages and points to a diet the like of which I can only ponder.

He did, however, have a reputation for being somewhat fierce in the protection of his realm and his family. One neighbouring king who rejoiced in the name of Gwynllyw of Gwynllwg (who also became a saint) became enamoured of Brychans daughter, Gwladys (yet another saint) but his advances were refused and so saw no harm or compunction in kidnapping her. Brychan was furious and a battle was fought between the two which lasted over three days. It was, it has been said, only due to the intervention of the 'High King', no less a person than Arthur himself, that peace was restored and with it, presumably, the aforesaid Gwladys.

*Brecon Beacons*

Boudicca - Brecon

Adwen, Canauc (Cynog), Cleder (Clether), Dilic (Illick), Endelient (Endelienta), Helie, Johannes (Sion), Iona, Julianna (Ilud), Kenhender (Cynidr), Keri (Curig), Mabon (Mabyn), Menfre (Menefrewy), Merrewenne (Marwenna), Morewenna (Morwenna), Nectanus (Nectan), Tamalanc, Tedda (Tetha), Wencu (Gwencuff, Gwengustle), Nennocha, Wenheden (Enoder), Wenna (Gwen), Wensent, Wynup (Gwenabwy) and Yse (Issey).

Quite prolific!

Of the children listed as coming into Cornwall and leaving their names at places we can recognize today are:

Johannes at St Ive.

Endelient at St Endellion.

Menfre at St Minver.

Tedda at St Teath.

Mabon at St Mabyn.

Merewenne at Marhamchurch.

Wenna at St Wenn.

Keyne at St Keyne.

Yse at St Issey.

Morwenna at Morwenstow.

Cleder at St Clether.

Keri at Egloskerry.

Helie at Egloshayle.

Adwen at Advent.

Lanent at Lelant.

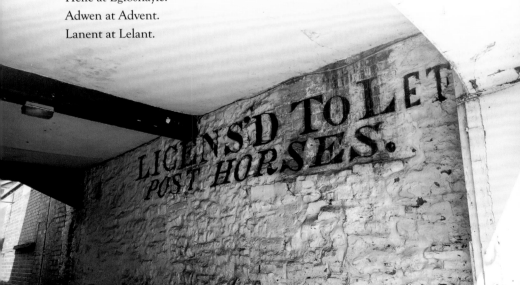

WELLINGTON

MDCCCLII

THIS STATUE MODELLED FROM LIFE
BY THE LATE JOHN EVAN THOMAS F.S.A. J.P.
DEPUTY LIEUTENANT AND HIGH SHERIFF
OF THE COUNTY OF BRECKNOCK
WAS PRESENTED BY HIM
TO HIS NATIVE TOWN IN THE YEAR 1856

*Welington - Brecon*

The list of his progeny is so prolific that an entire volume could be written on that subject alone.

We must, however, bear in mind as we continue our study that many of these must be associated children as opposed to his personal output of bloodline. It is inconceivable that one man could sire this amount of offspring in his lifetime.

To complete this list of children we must however add the list from the Irish records who have Brychan marrying a certain Dina who was the daughter of the King of the Saxons:

Mo-Goroc.
Mo-Chonoc.
Diraid.
Duban (Dyfnan).
Cairinne (Caian).
Cairpre.
Iast.
Elloc (Dilic).
Paan.
Caeman.
Mo-Beoc.

There is also a tradition in Brittany that Brychan also married Menedoc who was the daughter of King Constantine of the Scots and together they were the parents of Nennocha. (Just the one there then)!

It is without doubt the size of the attributed family that gives such rise to the legends of 'saintly' proclivity of Brychan and his children. As with any family of great reputation many would want to be related to them and equally as many would be attributed after death owing to their virtues during life. The vast majority of Brychan's children, including Brychan himself, were later to be elevated to 'Sainthood' and as we have seen, many of them were left to posterity in place names in and around Cornwall and the West Country.

Of all of these children however, be they real or attributed, there are four who deserve special mention due to their importance in Cornwall. Of these four we have already heard of St Nectan. That leaves us with:

Clether. We believe Clether lived mostly as a hermit and originated in Wales and lived originally by the River Never. Moving to Cornwall Clether settled in the Inny Valley where his name is still born at the place attributed to his cell. His first cell had an oratory added later and this together with his well became a major site for pilgrimage. We believe St Clether might also be the same person as St Cleer who is associated with another cell and shrine in a small village just south of the Inny Valley. His feast day is 4th November.

Endellion.

She could also be Endelient who is listed as one of Brychan's children. In St Endleion in Cornwall part of her tomb and two wells survive.

Also a chapel was named after her in Tregony where she is also reputed to have stayed regularly.

While she stayed at Tregony she is reputed to have lived on only the milk of one cow which unfortunately strayed onto the lands of a local lord who promptly killed the cow. The lord we are told then mysteriously died but was miraculously restored to life by St Endellion. Her feast day is 29th April.

Last, but by no means least, is St Morwenna. Also, perhaps called Mwynen and sometimes confused with St Modwenna. She is patron of Morwenstow and according to the legends the local people grew enormously fond of her and decided to build her a chapel. In her attempt to help Morwenna carried a large rock on her head from the bottom of the quarry being used and when she got close to the site where the chapel was built she dropped it and at thatvery spot a spring flowed from the ground and became sacred to her memory. Her feast day is 5th July.


**To summarize then:**

Brychan, later St Brychan, came from Ireland to settle in Wales. *Possible.*
Brychan sired over sixty children. *Improbable.*
Many of the associated children were elevated to sainthood. *Fact.*
A large number of the children left their names in Cornwall. *Fact.*
The accompanying pilgrim trail became prolific. *Fact.*
Cornwall appears to host more saints than most counties. *Fact.*

Brecon Beacons

# POOLS, WELLS AND LOST HEADS

So far we have looked at numerous saints and their place in association with Nectan and other Dark Age luminaries. Now, I feel we can spend some time investigating other sites and saints that have relevance when we talk on the subject of 'Sacred Springs and Wells'.

We have certainly seen that Cornwall is possibly more blessed than any other county in Britain with the proliferation of sacred sites dealing with holy waters and healing springs but there are just one or two worth mentioning, still situated in the West Country, that deserve their place in this book.

Of these sites both are situated in Somerset and both have achieved a status in Britain fitting to their purpose. They both tell the stories of saints whose cults became pre-eminent during the middle-ages but have remained popular up to the present time. This dignity is, I feel, one that Nectan deserves. So, first let me deal with:

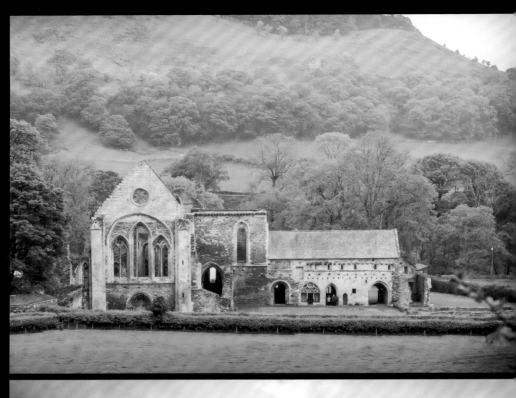

Vale Crucis Abbey - Llangollen

# SAINT AUDREY

**S**aint Audrey, who is sometimes referred to as 'Saint Etheldreda' also occupies that time in our history labelled the dark Ages.

She was, it is said, the foundress of Ely Cathedral in the county of Cambridgeshire. As you approach the 'fens' you see Ely rising up from the flat marshes like a huge sentinel and the cathedral is surmounted by a vast multi-facetted tower that looks down on the marshes it has dominated for centuries.

She was by birth of a great noble family and her father was none other than Anna, King of the East Anglians. We believe she was probably born at Exning in Suffolk.

However, it's Audrey's travels into the west that will spark our interest. According to legend, or at least one version of them, she was promised in marriage to a war-lord who resided in Somerset and the gentleman was not, as we believe, a good catch. In fact his capacity for violence was second to none and any young lady being unfortunate enough to land him in wedlock would very soon be a suitable case for treatment!

Rather than allow herself to be tied to this man Audrey loudly proclaimed that not only was she not going to marry him but, and most importantly, she had promised herself to God and was desirous of becoming a 'Holy Sister' and taking the robes as a bride of Christ.

If we follow the legend it tells us that he was so enraged he cut her head off and where it landed a sacred spring gushed forth. Now that, of course, should be the end of the story, however, strolling along the lane and witnessing this was her uncle, Saint Collum, who had a cell and abbey in Llangollen in North Wales. Having watched the incident he picked her head up and placed it back on her shoulders and she miraculously rose fit and well.

The site of this act is celebrated at 'Audrey's Head' near Watchett in North Somerset. It actually became so popular and so very quickly that it boasts the reputation of being one of the first real tourist attractions in Britain with the attendant souvenirs being sold.

The souvenirs themselves have their place in history as they were all loc-ally made by inhabitants who wished, quite logically, to make a littlebusiness opportunity out of the shrine at the spring. Small wooden dolls were made and these were gaudily painted and had cheap cloth attached to them to represent

*Vale Crucis Abbey - Llangollen*

Audrey's vestments. The paint quickly peeled off and the cheap cloth equally as quickly became detached from the dolls. Anything that fell into the same bracket as these shoddy trinkets became known as a 'Saint Audrey' and from these early tourist souvenirs we get the term 'Tawdry' which rightly describes anything of a shoddy nature!

As for her uncle, Saint Collum, the great 'Vale Crucis Abbey' at Llangollen is his testament to history.

Well, so much for legend. But there is certainly a history we can attach to Audrey that is rather less colourful but equally as interesting.

Born in Exning, as we have seen, it is listed that she actually married at an early age (in 652) to Tondberht, an ealdorman of South Gyrwas. She remained though a virgin during the marriage and we believe that this was due to her early years at marriage and the ealdorman's advancing years. He died in 655 and she retired to Ely which was actually her dowry in marriage so the land was now hers.

In 660 she was wedded to the young King of Northumbria, Egfrith, who at 15 was much younger then Audrey. Part of the bargain, as it was a political marriage, was that Audrey should keep her virginity. After 12 years of marriage Egfrith wanted to consummate the marriage (he had afterall waited 12 years bargain or not) but Audrey (Etheldreda) and the Bishop of Northumbria, Wilfrid, advised young Egfrith against this. He tried bribing her with gifts but all

Vale Crucis Abbey - Llangollen

to no avail. She left him and went to Coldingham were her aunt, Saint Ebbe, was abbess and became a nun under her tuition.

She then founded the great abbey at Ely in 673 and Egfrith married again and, for his troubles, Wilfrid was exiled from Northumbria.

It is said she was joined by her sisters and nieces who made up the body of the church there and finally in 679 she died of a tumour on the neck. Ah, here comes the 'head' bit. They said at the time that her neck tumour was God's punishment for her wearing necklaces during her youth, infact it was the plague and would also, eventually, carry off many of her sisters.

Seventeen years after her entombment in the abbey, her shrine was opened and her body was not only found to be incorrupt but the tumour on the neck had healed. Obviously this was a sign of sanctity and Audrey/Etheldreda found her way into the book of the sanctified.

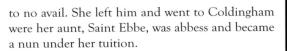

*Vale Crucis Abbey - Llangollen*

The placing of Joseph of Arimathea in Britain had been firmly identified (in legend) as the 1st century AD.

The quite fabulous story tells us that Joseph was a merchant, in fact a tin merchant, and he frequently visited these shores sailing with Phoenician crews in his merchant vessels to deal with the inhabitants of Britain. This much is quite feasible. Local legend now takes over the story.

It is reputed that Joseph was the uncle of Jesus of Nazareth and that, as the wealthy uncle, it is possible that he brought the boy Jesus with him on his travels. It has been argued as a possibility as the boyhood of Jesus is not documented at all and it was quite common for the wealthier relative to take the young off-spring of poorer relatives with them on business trips. Yes, that much is arguably a possibility. So much so that it was reported that the first 'wattle' hut in Glastonbury that would later be the heart of the great abbey there was reputed to have been built by the boy Jesus' own hands.

Even our great poet William Blake would immortalize this in his towering anthem "And Did Those Feet In Ancient Time" (often wrongly called 'Jerusalem' which is in fact the name of the tune to which it is played).

According to the story and local belief, after the crucifixion Joseph is said to have landed in Britain (in a part he already knew well) and came with his wife and twelve followers and their wives. Around the wattle building that was built, it is said, by the boy Jesus on his earlier travels, Joseph and his followers built a circle of wattle huts in which to live with the old central hut being used for liturgical purposes (thus making it the first Christian church above ground in the world).

By the side oh of the wattle hut was a natural well which, in due course, was built into the fabric of the building of the abbey in the 'Lady Chapel' which occupied the site of the original wattle building, known now to history as the 'Vetusta Ecclesia'. Named 'Saint Joseph's Well' it still occupies the same place and can be seen by any visitor to the abbey church. The well played an important part in the liturgy of the abbey and even now still holds a spell over those who see it.

Whereas the well in the abbey has its place in our quest perhaps the well that is most associated with the Glastonbury legends is that of the 'Chalice Well' which lies a short distance from the abbey in Chilkwell Street.

The Chalice Well and its gardens have become something of a 'Mecca' for visitors and pilgrims of both the Christian and Pagan paths owing to its mystery and the beauty of its setting. As you enter the grounds you soon discover that the well is, in fact, on three different levels with a spiritual garden enclosure assigned to each level.

The Chalice Well - Glastonbury

One of the first things that you notice as you enter the area is the startling blood red colour of anything that the water has flown over and onto for any period of time, a truly magical effect that is explained in a scientific way by the fact that the water is very heavy with natural iron deposits. This has also given rise to its alternative name of the 'Blood Spring'.

The first and indeed the largest you come across is the front pool which is fed by a carefully designed waterfall that feeds it. The design of the pool is that which is known as a 'Vesica Pisces' and shows two pools interlinked.

Each part of the pool overlaps and describes, in its design, two perfect circles with an ellipse at the point of intersection. This has been said to be an interpretation of the meeting of this world and the next or even the joining point with our world and the Celtic 'Other World' that exists alongside our own.

The design was executed by the architect Frederick Bligh-Bond who was, for some period, responsible for the archaeological excavations at the abbey.

The design can also be interpreted as being the form of the 'Divine Feminine' that form of the Goddess worshipped by so many. The falls which feed the pool are of an intriguing form as they show the water being dispensed by falling from one bowl into another as it makes it way down into the pool below. This first pool is where many pilgrims come to leave their offerings or, indeed, their crystals or other personal items for a type of re-energizing that the water is supposed to impart on any item left in it.

The next section one comes to is the 'Lions Head' and it is here that it is possible to take the water from the cups provided. The flow of the water is constant, as is its temperature. The flow never varies and is always present for any visitor. In this part of the gardens it is also reported that if taking photographs strange phenomena can effect the film being used (this is also true of the modern digital camera), many people have reported such effects

The Chalice Well - Glastonbury

as a rainbow appearing on the photograph just above the 'Lions Head' and others have shown misty shapes standing to the side of the small pool that the lion feeds into. This can be personally attested to by myself as well as countless others as photographs have shown, on occasion, varying phenomena at this point of the 'Well Gardens'.

The third and last section you attain is the 'Well Head' itself. This section of the gardens is set aside for private prayer and contemplation. The well head comprises of a stone surround set with many ammonite fossils and raised above it is a well cover. The covering of the well head itself echoes the design of the Vesica Pisces and upon closer inspection you will see at thispoint that the two circles are intersected by a spear. Again there are more than one explanation for this design. Being an emblem of the Divine Feminine the spear as it pierces through the centre of the symbol is emblematic of the male and female elements that exist for all living things to exist. It is also redolent of yet another part of the legend of Joseph of Arimathea. We are told that Joseph brought with him, when he arrived at Glastonbury, the Holy Grail (whatever that might have been) as it is said it might be the cup used at the Last Supper or even the bowl that Joseph used at the Crucifixion to catch the blood and water that flowed from the side of Jesus of Nazareth as he was fixed upon the Cross.

He is also said, according to legend and local belief, to have brought with him

*The Chalice Well - Glastonbury*

two cruets of finely wrought silver and one was said to hold the divine blood and one the water from the wound (they having miraculously not combined but remained separate) and deposited these treasures in his new house of worship which became the abbey. At his death, however, it is said that these items were buried with him in a secret place, this place being the Chalice Well, hence its name. The reality of these legends cannot, of course, be proved but they add to the mystery and, some would say, the sanctity of a site as if we could prove everything would there be any room for faith in belief?

The White Spring - Glastonbury

Just outside the gardens there is, in another building which is varyingly a shop or tea room, another spring but this is of the chalk variety and where many think that Chilkwell Street might be derived from 'Chalice Well Street' it is equally possible that it could hail from 'Chalk Well Street' and, in fact, refer to the lesser of the two springs that occupy this part of Glastonbury.

The Chalice Well - Glastonbury

Having looked at these two and highly important sites I believe it would now be a good time in our journey to return to Cornwall and

The Chalice Well - Glastonbury

look at some of the lesser known but, to my mind at least, equally as important wells and springs of the county. We must bear in mind that simply because a particular site has not had the benefit of medieval 'spin' or modern marketing it would be improper to consign that well/spring and its attendant saint to oblivion as not being worthy of note.

I believe it would only be right to start of with one of Cornwall's best loved saints and ,indeed, a sister of our own dear Nectan, Saint Morwenna.

Obviously being a sister of Nectan she automatically is listed as one of the prolific family of Brychan. When we look at the early saints and followers of the Celtic church we really are looking at people with incredible tenacity yet lone, in many cases, astonishing bravery.

Morwenna, it is said, was fired by a desire to follow her brother and assist in evangelizing the Cornish. Leaving her home with her father and many siblings in Wales we are told she ventured forth toward Cornwall, navigating the waters that separate the two countries in nothing but a coracle! For those of you have not come across one of these craft before please allow to me describe a coracle to you. It is a small boat, normally made of a wooden superstructure and circular, again normally about six feet or so across. The structure is covered with treated and proofed hides more often than not and is steered by one person using a simple paddle. This paddle is used by leaning toward the front of the vessel and stroking the paddle alternately to the left and right in short sweeping gestures (If you attempt to 'row' you succeed only in going around in circles). Using this small and flimsy craft then was how Morwenna arrived at the most northerly point of Cornwall at a place now called Morwenstow.

*St John's Church - Morwenstow*

At the site she chose for her cell or hermitage and later where her church was built by her parishioners, she found a clear spring flowing from a natural source in the nearby slate. Not only, of course, was this of use as a supply of sweet water but would also prove invaluable for liturgical purposes. Since its inception the act of baptism has been vital to the accepted church. The whole ritual of being baptized is central to the basic tenets of the faith.

We looked briefly at the legend of Morwenna earlier but she is worthy of re-mentioning due to her closeness to her brother Nectan.

Morwenna spent much of her time at her chosen home near to the cliffs on that remarkable coast line. On clear days it would have been possible for her to see her previous home in South Wales, distant enough and yet close enough to afford her comfort in times of need.

Nectan was said to have been with her at the time of passing and it is said she asked to look again across the coast to look once more on Wales.

Visiting her well at Saint Morwenna's even to this day the modern pilgrim will notice that it still faces out toward the Welsh side of the Severn Sea.

The well is well kept and housed in a slate structure with a firm roof and built into the hillside with skilful artisan hands.

After her death her cult grew rapidly. Pilgrims regularly came to visit her church and well (the spring that she chose to dwell by) and as her popularity grew so, of course, did the reputation of the local area. Any place that boasted a 'holy' personage or, indeed, a saint could be sure that its own revenue would benefit from the attending business.

St Morwenna's Well - Morwenstow

If one looks at Shrewsbury with its beautiful and yet small abbey, we can trace the growth of the town due to its holding the shrine of Saint Winifred.

She had two sites, one at Holywell and the other in the town. As the shrine resided inside the abbey so around the walls of the abbey stall holders would erect their tables and shelters for the selling of wares to the pilgrims. Also, the local hostelries would benefit greatly providing accommodation to the pilgrims who could afford it.

As an interesting point, there are many towns and cities that have ancient buildings either within or just outside their boundaries that are denoted as 'Hospitals'. These were not hospitals of the modern medical type but were suppliers of 'hospitality' to the traveller and the distressed.

St Morwenna's Well - Morwenstow

A very fine example exists in the medieval city of Lichfield just (originally) outside the walls of the city. The Hospital Of Saint John Baptist was founded in the 11th century to provide succour and comfort for the pilgrim visiting the shrine of Saint Chad located in the cathedral. Comfort would be given to the poor traveller as well as those who were locked outside the city gates after curfew. The hospital now provides a refuge for the elderly and its buildings are amongst the most lovely in the Midlands.

St Morwenna's Well - Morwenstow

St Neot's Well - Poundstock

# Saint Neot's Well, Poundstock

This saint we know died in, or around, 877 AD. He is attributed to St. Neot in Cornwall and also to St. Neots in Cambridgeshire.

In the early years of his religious calling he joined the community of Glastonbury Abbey in Somerset which was certainly a place where many men of a holy disposition were attracted to. It was, after all, one of the largest and, according to legend, the most ancient of religious houses in Britain.

It was from there that he travelled to Cornwall and settled near Bodmin Moor to take up life as a hermit. Many of the religious persuasion tended to be attracted to the more desolate parts of the country as they felt with the solitude that comes with desolation the remoteness lends itself to the perfecting of the soul away, as it is, from the temptations and distractions of normal daily life.

Even today many people, myself included, have found that going 'on retreat' to one of the many religious houses or communities that offer such services can help to clear the mind and soul of any clutter and detritus that may be distracting us from our higher purpose (if that is we can allow ourselves the luxury of having a higher purpose)!

St. Neot's Well, Poundstock

When Neot settled in Bodmin he founded a small monastery. After a while deciding to forsake the solitary life and gathering to himself men of a similar path at a place then to be called Neotstoke (now St. Neot). After his death his relics were placed in his shrine in the church at the North end by the sanctuary. It was the custom in most churches, in due time, for a small 'chantry chapel' to be built enclosing the shrine and in here the mass could be said for the benefit of the people (or sometimes just those who paid for the erection of the chapel), but suffice to say it drew its pilgrims from far and near.

There was however a danger if you were an establishment that held the relics of any saint and that was envy. Many stories remain that have been authenticated by fact throughout history that the relics of saints were sometimes 'loaned' for want of a better phrase and never returned and often simply blatantly stolen, frequently not without violence. This fate happened to the bones of dear Neot.

We are reliably informed that in or around the year 972 Earl Alfric founded an abbey at Eynesbury in Cambridgeshire with some of the community from Thorney. It was said that via the warden of Neot's in Cornwall they obtained the gift of almost all of Neot's bones. This is highly unlikely as it would seriously detract from the wealth and status of the Cornish abbey to allow such a thing and far more likely that the relics were obtained by more underhand methods. It is said that the Cambridgeshire shrine housed all of Neot's relics save for one arm and that the relics were investigated and classed as genuine by no

*St Neot's Well - Poundstock*

St Neot's Well - Poundstock

*Poundstock Gildhouse*

less a personage than St. Anselm himself. To the community at the priory of Bec Anselm granted a cheekbone from these relics and thus ensured their own fortune for pilgrims.

Any visitor to Poundstock is going to enjoy the walk to this ancient and venerable shrine. Lying as it does just beyond the town of Bude it has a superb church and most excellent 'Gildhouse' of great antiquity. It is believed to date from the 14th century and was built, it is said, to house the masons who were working on the construction of the church. There is another holy well standing about half a mile away, however it this site that tends to captivate the pilgrim. St. Neot was said to be of tiny stature and would recite the gospels whilst standing immersed up to his neck in the cold waters. I think this must be what they mean by 'mortification of the soul'.

Indeed, there have been many followers of the religious or holy path that have deemed it necessary to endure the most extreme privations of discomfort in order, they believe, to achieve a true spiritual awareness.

Suffering would be, it would seem, fundamental to some who follow this path. Hair shirts, fasting, extreme cold, self flagellation, and total silence all these and more have been adopted by the seeker of the holy truth.

St Winwaloe - Poundstock

St Winwaloe - Poundstock

# SAINT PIRAN

It would be wrong not to include this eminent saint as he is, after all, patron saint of Cornwall. Once again, we appear to be dealing with a man of Irish/Welsh descent very similar to that of Nectan. What is more they appear to be living in near time proximity to one another as Piran did not die until the year 480.

He gave his name, of course, to Perranporth (or Piran's Port) on the coast.

His well is actually situated very close to that of Nectan at Trethevy and is alongside the old pilgrims way. The well head itself is again of good Cornish slate and stone and has a stout metal grid-type gate to keep it safe. The water that flows in it appears to emanate from a hollow rock set deep inside its structure and it is believed by some that the water flows over the remains of the saint himself lying concealed inside its recesses.

Saint Piran is also the Patron saint of Cornish Miners. His flag, which is also the Cornish national flag, shows a white cross on a black-ground and this is said to represent the tin issuing forth from the dark mines and whereas some would say that, in times of danger of imminent collapse down a mine, the 'knockers', or Cornish mine sprites, would be heard tapping away on the walls to warn the miners to escape, it was also said it was Piran tapping to ensure a safe deliverance of the Cornish men.

near St Piran's Well - Trethevy

St Piran's Church - Trethevy

St Piran's Church - Trethevy

St Piran's Church - Trethevy

St Piran's Well - Trethevy

St Piran's Church - Trethevy

St Piran's Well - Trethevy

St Piran's Church - Trethevy

Jetwells Well - Camelford

# JETWELL'S HOLY WELL

ow this one, as far as origin is concerned, can be a little confusing. It could easily be that this well derives its name from Saint Juliot, a very obscure saint, again dating from the 5th century and yet again said to be one of Brychan's daughters! Her name also appears as Ilud and Juliana. She can certainly lay claim to a church and cross dedicated to her at Luxulyan in Cornwall. Like her 'brother' Nectan, she is supposed to have been robbed and instead of seeking temporal justice sought instead to convert the propagator of the theft into the path of virtue and was promptly, and very violently, killed by said villain.

She has sometimes been confused with St. Julitta as she has a chapel which can be seen, in foundations only, at Tintagel Castle. However, the confusion does not stop there as the original dedication of the chapel might have been to St. Juliot.

There is no actual feast day for her in the saint's calendar but in Tintagel, which is her parish , they keep a feast day for her on the closest Sunday to June 29th.

Jetwells Holy Well lies close to Camelford and Lanteglos. As with most of the sacred wells that exist this one is no exception as to having healing properties, particularly for those suffering from skin conditions and, it is said, that bathing in its waters will cure those suffering from any skin-born malady.

The well itself was very nearly lost for all time as during the 19th century the surrounding stones, many of which were carved with holy images, were unceremoniously ripped from the well housing and cast down into the well as the stones were seen to be hazardous to cattle! Help was at hand however by virtue of one Colonel Bake who, learning of the fate of the well, restored order as best he could and now, although it is a little remote, the well stands again for visitors. It must be said however that what the visitor sees is not the original site of the well but the stones being re-housed as it were and the 'well' now stands dry but still, by association, worthy of a visit to venerate this charming but little known saint.

# SAINT CLETHER

et another child of Brychan. As with other of his siblings Clether, Cleer or Clanis, is said to have originally come to Cornwall from Wales again possibly following his elder brother Nectan. It would seem he started his religious calling in his native Wales and had settled near the river Never. It was from here that he ventured forth into Cornwall and came to rest at the lovely Inny valley. He had an oratory and well there and they were renowned for their beauty and pilgrims soon came to place Clether's shrine high on the list of places to which the pilgrim trail would take them.

The well and oratory seen now were rebuilt in the 14th century and are remarkable examples of their type. He also gave his name to the village of Cleer which is situated a few miles to the south.

At the well chapel it is possible to see a huge granite monolith altar that is said to have remained in situ since the shrine was first built. Little is known of his life and it is not uncommon for him to be over-looked by those who are on their quest but I believe he is worth including here by virtue of the fact that he is akin to our Nectan and contemporary to much of what was happening in Britain at this time.

Close by to St. Clethers is situated Laneast. The well here is near to the church and is, by today's standards and quite surprisingly, in remarkably good condition. The well housing stands above a clear spring that sheds its water into the marsh lands that spread below it. Again, the front of the well is protected by a large and well studded oaken door to prevent the profane from despoiling its interior in much the same way it always has.

# Rialton Priory Well

This priory was once at the centre of a thriving community called 'Royal Town' which traced its history certainly back to the time of the noble Black Prince, or Edward of Woodstock, the hero of the 'Hundred Years War'. The monastic community that settled here did so , we believe, as a retreat and were originally part of the brethren of St. Petroc's in Bodmin. Again, it's fair to assume that this well, seated over its spring, was once part of the liturgical need of the priory.

It is always fair to assume that if you have a well building on the property that is going to be a regular fixture, however, during the 19th century a rather singular occurrence took place. The then steward of the priory decided to move to Somerset but had become so fond of the well that he thought he would take it with him. It was removed stone by stone and brick by brick and rebuilt in his new home. When the authorities heard of this a very dim view was taken as you can imagine and it was demanded the well was reinstated post haste. This was duly done and now the well stands proud and in remarkable condition in the grounds of the old priory, now a private residence.

# Saint Pedyr's Well

Not far from Rialton Priory stands St. Pedyr's Well in much the same state it has enjoyed for centuries. The well house lies embedded into the slope behind it and before it stands a long and narrow pool that appears to be surrounded by a tiered enclosure. It could be that this was contrived to assist the pilgrim who come for some form of healing to do with foot problems or indeed simply to aid the foot weary traveller.

St. Pedyr is one of the most obscure saints from the dark ages and little or nothing is known of his life but a visit to the well invokes images of the early Christianity in Cornwall and those legendary times before the Norman invasion.

# HOLYWELL BAY

**H**olywell Bay also falls into the category of Obscure but incredibly beautiful. It holds a unique quality all its own as it lies hidden in a cavern near the shore line. Holywell Bay is quite close to Newquay but to approach it is a quest in itself.

Before even starting on the journey it's wise to check on the times of the tides for that region. To achieve your goal it's necessary to negotiate the sand-dunes and then to travel up the length of the beach until you see before you some caves, then take a moment to make sure that you have chosen correctly. When you enter the cave that holds the 'well' you will first notice a water cascade just inside the cave that streams forth and stains the rocky interior. At the very depth of the cave is a small cavern that heavily drips with water.

Here at last is the site you have been searching. It was the custom for mothers to bring their children here on November 1st (The Celtic Samhain festival) and pass them through the cleft there into the water to be healed, particularly of ailments affecting their limbs. Whereas the cave is beset by the sea and its saltwater issue the cavern itself holds fresh, clear water and this was that which the parents would use for their sickly children and, if sources are to be believed, with great efficacy.

aint Breward, again, appears to have been of Welsh origin and we can date him to the 6th century. He is also named as Branwalader, Branwalator and Brelade.

He was certainly of the Celtic church and it is believed that he was a monk who later in his life might have been elevated to the rank of bishop. He is said to have worked closely with St. Samson both in Cornwall and the Channel Islands and quite possibly in Brittany as well.

He is reported to have been a son of a Cornish king, perhaps with a Welsh mother? During the 10th century King Athelstan was said to have obtained his relics from monks in Brittany and had them enshrined in his own monastery at Milton in Dorset. We believe however that the relics might have constituted just his head. It was quite common practice for a saints head to be removed after death and kept as a separate relic. This holds true in many areas. In the cathedral of Lichfield in Staffordshire there exists in the thickness of the south wall an entrance to a staircase. The stair climbs through the thickness of the masonry and opens out into a quite beautiful little chapel, the chapel of 'St. Chad's Head'. Chad is the patron saint of Lichfield and his shrine was just behind the high altar and choir. A modernized shrine can still be seen there and votives are still made to Chad at this point but the original was dismantled during the dissolution of the 16th century.

In the chapel of his head however there is in the side wall by the altar a locked cupboard door into the brickwork and it was in here that St. Chad's head was kept and on his feast day of March 2nd his skull was held out over the knave for the pilgrims to venerate. It's pleasing to note that, for the benefit of visiting school children, a replica is kept and displayed in such a manner for them.

At the rear of the cathedral, over the 'Minster Pool' stands St. Chad's church in its grounds you can still see the covered well in which he is said to have baptised the local Saxons.

To return to St. Breward, his well can be found down a lane at Chapel Farm and it remains still sturdy with its walls and archway still firm in Cornish stone.

St Guron's Well - Bodmin

St. Petroc's Church - Bodmin

# Saint Guron's Well

**S**aint Guron, sometimes called Gyron, was yet another, we believe, who originally called Wales his home. A 6th century religious man and also a mystic he is said to have arrived into Cornwall ahead of St. Petroc and it was Guron who spearheaded his particular type of evangelizing.

Most of our saints have been listed as being of the Celtic persuasion and, indeed, they were at the forefront of preaching the new faith in Britain. The Roman church arriving later and, at times, to much consternation!

When Guron arrived near Bodmin he set about erecting a tall standing stone.

This might have been adorned with carvings of sacred motifs and near to this was the well he dedicated to the new Lords service. We are told, in legend, that he fasted for forty days and nights to prepare himself for this dedication.

This might even give us a clue as to the time scale we are looking at, this might have been 'Lent'?

The local people actually quickly took to Guron and a settlement quickly grew around his cell and well. This would in time become one of the pre-eminent monasteries in all of Cornwall.

The well itself stands near the western door of St. Petroc's church and is high roofed and again possesses a door to protect it from the vernacular. The well head sports two carved stone gargoyle heads that exude the spring water. It's worth remembering that a carved head is only a true gargoyle if it is used for the passage of water (drainpipes etc) if it is merely a carved head it should be described as a 'grotesque'.

St. Petroc's Church (old) - Bodmin

St. Petroc's Church - Bodmin

St. Guron's Well - Bodmin

St. Petroc's Church - Bodmin

# TRELIL WELL

**T**relil is situated near to Wendron and it is the home to a particular well of some interesting lineage.

To the east of Helston lies a valley that has a bright stream that passes through it and at the bottom of a pasture in this valley is the well we seek. It comprises of a good stone building and inside it there are even seats of a ledge type.

The well is dedicated to St. Wendronas who, it is said gave name to Wendron which lies close by. However, if we research we will actually see that the original dedication was to St. Ia. Ia, also known as Hya and Ives was, of course, patron saint of St. Ives.

Irish by birth it is said she sailed over to take up a religious life in Cornwall.

The historian Leland tells that she was actually a disciple of St. Baricus and that her first church was built under instruction of Dinan who held a great postion in Cornwall and was one of its premier lords. In Brittany there is a tradition that she arrived there at the head of 777 followers and was martyred there dying a virgin!

We do know that associated with the well, however, is a charming legend whicht states that a church was to be built over the site where the well now stands but every night when the builders went home the crows and ravens came and dismantled their work brick by brick until they gave up and built the church in Wendron where it now stands. Perhaps this is Ia not allowing another saint to encroach on her well?

**We will finish with:**

# SANCREED

ancreed stands in the south of Corwall not far from Penzance. The reason for including this is the because I believe it to be what it always has been and that is strictly pagan water shrine! The exact placing of the well is now known as Chapel Downs but the well itself appears never to have been used for any liturgical purposes whatever. It stands in a grove of ancient pine and holly and exudes a strange will as if it were in control of the surrounding area and you are there because it wants you to be. This is an unearthly little well and rather charming for that.

It has been noted by Cheryl Straffon in her superb book Fentynyow Kernow, (see the book list at the end), that the water has been registered as being 200% background of radiation count. That would certainly be deemed ripe for visions if taken regularly.

The summary for this chapter will be included in the text of the final chapter when, I hope and trust, I pull together all the reins we have loosed into one cohesive statement which will give more clarity to your personal quest.

*Sancreed Holy Well : Sancreed*

St Creden - Sancreed

Behind Sancreed Holy Well - Sancreed

Sancreed Holy Well - Sancreed

St Creden - Sancreed

*Davidstow Parish Church - Davidstow*

# Davidstow Church and Well, Another of Cornwall's many churches with wells close by St Clether's

*Davidstow Holy Well - Davidstow*

*Inside the well - Davidstow*

*Roman Town - Wroxeter*

# THE LEGACY OF THE DRAGON

 his chapter, the penultimate, will, I think, throw open a new doorway onto Saint Nectan and the ever long and confusing topic of the real 'King' Arthur.

When we look at any of the legends or history surrounding 'Arthurian' Britain it is necessary to go back further in history than the actual dawning of the character himself. Many historical occurrences gave rise to his being, whether in legend or fact, these must be dealt with if only as briefly as this book will allow.

Britain had, for many centuries, been part of the Roman Empire, but what does that actually mean? How did we function as part of an empire hundreds of miles away.

When the might of Rome finally arrived in Britain, subduing the local people they brought with them a number of things. ("What have the Romans ever done for us"?). First and foremost they brought the army, the most perfect killing machine in Europe at the time. The legions were the best trained and equipped fighting troops during that period, 50 BC to 300 AD. (Approximately).

Interestingly at the start of Rome's quest for an empire it was the foot troops

*The Wrekin - Shropshire*

that won the day as, then, the cavalry was made up mainly of the sons of nobles and the upper middle classes and were largely ineffectual in combat.

It would be into the late 1st century before the Roman cavalry would gain the reputation they would carry for centuries and that would involve the input of distinctly non-Roman people.

Wherever Rome conquered they brought with them and installed the Roman culture and, of course, the Roman 'civil service'. There can be little doubt that when Rome took over a country it put into place a system of structure that even since has rarely been equalled. Yes, Rome could be brutal in its treatment of conquered people, yes, its imperial families left a lot to be desired as far as sanity was concerned, (who can forget the emperor that married his favourite horse and had it proclaimed a God?). However, its commissariat was second to none (shouldn't that be 'nuli secundus?') and the attendant trades all benefited greatly.

One of the great bonuses of being conquered by Rome was that if you joined either the occupying army or its civil service it gave you one great advantage over your other countrymen who might not have followed this path, you became a citizen of Rome. That meant employment and, hugely importantly, a pension. For this reason in many of Rome's colonies you found they were manned by Rome's 'foreign legions', there were very few true Italian Romans throughout

the empire. After all, a country only has so many inhabitants, the great thing about Rome was how it spread its culture.

If we look at Britain as an example, here we had Spanish Romans, German Romans and even African Romans. When Geoffrey of Monmouth wrote his 'History of the Kings of Britain' it was taken, for many years, as a true history. Now however we know that he produced a medieval best seller by gleaning what he could of the history as it was known at the time and also combining legends. He spoke of Africa invading Britain! But if you go to you York you will see African tombstones, they were the Theban Legion of Rome that were garrisoned there. I always find it so fascinating to find out the small central 'gem' of a legend and to be able to put bones onto it.

The colonized inhabitants of countries that became part of the empire found that they adopted Roman culture rather more eagerly than we might expect.

When your area was settled you had cities, mettled roads, central heating, in fact, for many people they had 'never had it so good'!

Here in Britain we also took to the Roman cultural ethic. In the north of Britain the first line of defence was built, the Antonine Wall, short-lived as a defensive it might have been but a little further down when 'Hadrian's Wall' was built it was not just a wall to mark a line of military importance, it was far more. If we

*Roman Town - Wroxeter*

could have seen Hadrian's Wall when it was first built we would have seen, on the Scottish side, a line of fine masonry, well dressed in stone, and lime-washed to a brilliant finish. It was a political statement, here Rome was saying for all to see, 'Here is the edge of empire, here is the edge of civilization'! Rome's view on what constituted a barbarian became widely known, a barbarian is a nation that has no written culture. Actually rather unfair when you consider that here in Britain we were using the 'Ogham' alphabet. Obscure to non-Celts yes but still a fully functioning alphabet. Rome, however, brought its writing and language with it, Latin, the language of the civilized world.

A point worth remembering though is that Rome was not responsible for the building of the 'long straight' roads in this country, these roads already existed, or at least the majority of them, Rome however improved them tremendously, that has to be said. Again, where the army went it also had its own civil engineers, the roads, cities, etc would have to be built and be built quickly and well.

Another ruse of Rome for good government, (at least in Rome's view) was to keep the old tribal boundaries of the country, if you keep the country divided it makes it difficult for any resistance to be organized.

A similar method of governing was adopted by Britain when we made India part of our own growing empire, that states were kept independent with their own princes' et al but all answerable to the governors and the Viceroy. In much the same way that Rome would affect Britain with its culture, with the local 'Romans' being more Roman than the invaders, an identical situation occurred with the Anglo Indians who always thought of themselves as English and would often talk about "We British" and "Going home" when very few had or would ever leave India. So in Britain the Romano-Celt would become a hybrid of the two nations with Rome's culture being pre-eminent in its world.

During the period of interest, as far as this book is concerned, the most influential Romans who would have such an impact on us were another 'foreign' legion from Rome. These particular people would journey from the east of Europe to take post in Britain.

An ancient and noble tribe, we must talk of 'tribes' as 'clan' is actually quite a modern word, the Alani hailed from an area that had settled lands as far away as the Steppes. They were not only part of the Roman machine they were also bound to send young men into the army as 'tribute' from their nation, (in much the same way as an understanding was reached between ourselves and the noble Ghurkha troops from Nepal).

*Roman Town - Wroxeter*

been driven underground and was still worshipped by its followers in groves and woods wherever possible. The Romans had also introduced their own faiths into Britain, not only the native Gods and Goddesses of Rome itself but also, to some extent, the Gods and Goddesses of the countries of the 'naturalized'Romans. In Britain would have been seen the pantheon of Jupiter, Apollo, Daphne etc and also some of the tribal deities from all over Europe. One of the biggest cults to be followed was that of Mithras, the 'soldiers' God or Bull God of the Romans. His veneration would last until at least the 5th century in Britain and elsewhere.

When the Emperor Constantine was raised to the throne he introduced Christianity as the official religion of Rome, giving Christians finally respite from the centuries of persecution from Rome itself. This did cause a slight confusion though. Firstly, at this time there was a type of Christianity for virtually every country where it was known, Many variances on the central theme of 'Redemption' and the Crufixion. So when Constantine sent out his order and the order travelled all over the empire, by the time it arrived at the frontiers of the empire in far flung colonies like Britain the question was, "Is Christianity instead of or as well as"? Many places merely added images of Jesus of Nazareth onto their household altars together with their own effigies of the deities they had been worshipping for years. Confusing? Yes!

When the call came for Rome to leave Britain in the 4th/ 5th centuries it came because of the internal collapse of an empire that had not only over reached itself but was also suffering from many years of infighting that left the central structure weakened and its borders under threat, the greatest empire that the ancient world had known was coming to the end of its time in the form in which it had become known.

The legions began to withdraw and one by one its colonies were left to an existence strange to most of them. Now it was self government, apart from an appointed Roman representative, self regulation, self defensive (no more legions to call on) and, most importantly as far as Britain was concerned, the small separate kingdoms that made up the country were now left to look at their own borders. A power struggle ensued between the local 'kings' and warlords as to who would rule whom.

Each of the geographical areas looked with longing onto their neighbours, especially if natural resources were involved, to see if it was possible for that tribe to be subjugated and their wealth taken for their own. In an attempt to stabilize things after a period of time a 'High King' was took control but this did little to stop not only the petty land squabbles and outright piracy but also

Roman Town - Wroxeter

the increasing threat of incursion from the countries national frontiers.

The country was left with a strange hybrid community, a mismatch of people of whom some considered themselves Celt and some Roman (at least by adoption). As the legions had gone they had not only taken with them their military might but also the superstructure that ran the colony. The armourers, builders, engineers, leather workers, glaziers, masons, scribes, teachers, medical personnel all, or most, had left with the legions because that is where their loyalties lay and, of course, their livelihood. No legions and civil service, no pay.

The aftermath of this then was the world into which the man 'Arthur' and our St. Nectan were born into. A complex world of struggle and division, of new faiths and old ones, of warlords and priests, of legends and priestesses.

Britain, even then was a land worthy of winning, whether by a sword or by a God or Goddess, the land was a jewel that was struggling to maintain its presence and to ensure its survival.

During this period the primary source material available is, needless to say, quite scarce. There are some documents that give us a good picture of Britain at this time though and for this we must thank the men and women of the church. For centuries it had been the way of things that literacy was the provision of the church and, indeed, it would remain so for many centuries to come. Most teaching was provided not only to the novitiates but also to the children of nobility or those chosen very lucky few from ordinary walks in life by the monks who knew the written word. It is also a fact that the ancient Celtic oral tradition of keeping legends and histories were at this time starting to be written down for the first time.

Of these sources there are at least four that leap out as being of great interest.

The first would have to 'The Ruin Of Britain' by the monk St. Gildas. Here was a man who was writing about the internal fighting in Britain within living memory of the events, indeed I was St. Gildas who also ended his days in Brittany after the great exodus but more of that in a little while.

It is Gildas who first mentions the 'Great Dragon of the Island', if anything he is less than complimentary about any of the leaders of the time, describing them all as out for what they can get and all of them more interested in the pleasures of life and its rewards than the keeping of the kingdom.

In the 'Life' of St. Patrick we also have an account of a far from idyllic Britain. During the 8th century we have the History of Britain and the Annales

Cambriae or Welsh Annals. This gives a history, with some legend attached of Britain from 447-954. It is in the annals we first here of 'King' Arthur and also mention of a national catastrophe the , 'Days as dark as night' that may coincide with a cataclysmic seismic event in the Mediterranean which plunged much of Europe into a dark era of dust clouds and famine, this could easily be the starting point for the 'Waste Land' of the grail stories in which the land is classed as infertile due to a disaster which must be restored by the achieving of the grail.

It would appear that during this period of unrest certain of the people who decided to stay after Rome departed, such as the Alani still in the north and the loyal Votadini Celts, were asked to journey southwards and assist in areas of unrest where their skills as cavalrymen would be invaluable. Many of the northern Romano Celts stayed as they had intermarried with the locals and many were in fact 4th and even 5th generation of the original troops and settlers. Their great advantage was their expert horsemanship and this would prove invaluable in the years to come.

It was agreed that a large body of the northern folk would relocate to the Welsh marches, the land that incorporates the areas of the border counties including Shropshire, Herefordshire, Powys and other lands that were themselves in need of support and military intervention due to the local fighting and also, by this time, the threat of the Saxon incursion. The Saxons did not, as some people might think, merely decide to invade and take over the land for themselves. We have legendary evidence in the story of the perfidious Vortigern inviting over the Saxon warlords Hengist and Horsa to help in the quelling of tribal warfare in order that Vortigern could ensure his position as undisputed leader of Britain. The story then tells that he went back his arrangement to pay them and that they took matters into their own hands and simply seized what they wanted. The reality is, of course, a little different as some of the Saxons had been here in numbers for many years with many settling in the area around what we now call East Anglia and the lands around the south east coast and had become part of, during this time, become part of the community.

With arrival though of large forces intent on gaining land and fortune into more central areas of Britain it was soon found that Britain was now unprepared for such attacks and therefore help was needed. The northern troops of whom some were militia or reservist men and even some being paid mercenaries came down then and took up residence.

One of the prime sites for them to inhabit was the city of Viroconium now called Wroxeter which was at the time a major city in Roman Britain. Its placing made it ideal for the protection of the midlands the north and the area of the south west. It was also an ideal base for a military unit to strike out from and cause damage in a series of hit and run actions against the Saxon forces. Most sources appear to be telling of a leader called Arthur who fought trying to kick the Saxons out of Britain, I am of the opinion that he was, in fact, fighting a series of delaying actions to keep the Saxons from obtaining more land while a great number of the native population migrated into Brittany where a new realm was being founded, a realm that would continue the Celtic traditions of their previous land.

Gildas might have referred to this leader as the great 'Dragon' and that is surely as he would be seen. The dragon being the image of a great war commander, it was also the banners used by the troops in the north and its form would be seen in many of their fought struggles carried by a powerful warrior to protect it from falling into enemy hands in much the same way a regiments colours today symbolize not only the men but also their prowess in war.

Why then does a dragon become Arthur? The answer is not in a name but again a title. The name of the man is immaterial it is the knowledge you are facing the Arthur that matters. I use the prefix 'the' Arthur as it is in this

context, I believe, the warlord is known. Arthur is the 'Bear', that great beast of ferocity and power known and feared by all. It is, I believe, derived from the Roman term 'Ursa' meaning bear (as in Ursa Major and Ursa Minor) the Great and Little Bear in the constellations. If you ever journey to Tintagel in Cornwall make sure to visit the Great Halls of Arthur there in which you will find an astonishing display of stained glass, designed by Veronica Whall, that show the story of Arthur and the grail. One of the major windows shows the figure of the Merlin holding a star chart and upon it the constellation of the Great Bear, not by coincidence.

We would be looking at a man who would still have some remnants of Roman characteristics in uniform and certainly in military training and fighting methods. His mounted warriors would be seen as an elite body and very soon their reputation would spread far and wide as tales of the Arthur's prowess grew. To quote from Nennius:

"At that time the English increased their numbers and grew in Britain. On Hengist's death, his son Octha came down from the north of Britain to the kingdom of the Kentishmen, and from him are sprung the kings of the Kentishmen. The Arthur fought against them in those days, together with the

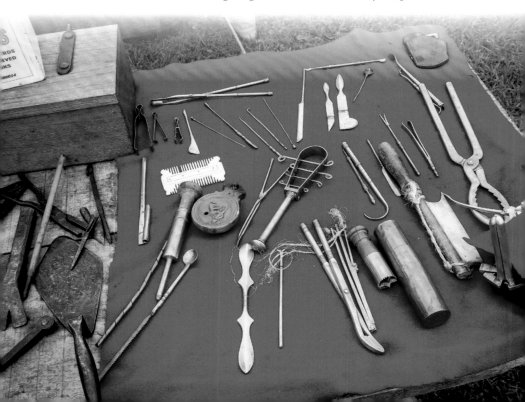

kings of the British; but he was their leader in battle.

The first battle was at the mouth of the river called Glein. The second, the third, the fourth and the fifth were on another river called the Douglas, which is in the country called Lindsey. The sixth battle was on the river called Bassas. The seventh battle was in the forest called Celyddon, that is, the Battle of Celyddon Coed. The eighth battle was in Guinnion fort, and I it Arthur carried the image of the holy Mary, the everlasting Virgin, on his shield and the heathen were put to flight that day, and there was a great slaughter upon them, through the power of our Lord Jesus Christ and the power of the Holy Virgin his mother. The ninth battle was fought in the city of the Legion. The tenth battle was fought on the bank of the river called Tryfrwyrd. The eleventh battle was on the hill called Agned. The twelfth battle was on Badon Hill and in it nine hundred and sixty men fell in one day, from a single charge of Arthur's, and no-one laid them low save he alone; and he was victorious in all his campaigns".

It is worth noting that the final battle 'Badon Hill' or Mons Badonicus', now thought to be at Bath in Somerset, was so successful that there was peace for forty years afterward, it seems that the threat of the Arthur was enough to keep the Saxons at bay.

The reason for some of the battles being so widespread is, I believe, down to keeping the Saxons busy on a wide frontier barrier and stop their advance. This was achieved by speed of movement of a chain of settlements that could be used for refuelling and fitting out men and horses. Possibly this would explain the fact that so many of the Iron Age hill forts were reused during this period, together with anything that Rome had left behind. With a central base at Wroxeter and a chain of the hill forts at his disposal the Arthur would have been able to use a 'Blitz Krieg' type of warfare. Hit quickly, hit hard and refuel.

A number of theories have been put forward as to the identity of the Arthur, many are worth studying as with information being at a premium for this historical period most is what we can term as 'educated theory' working with the information we have available to us at the time of writing. This also must come into that category. Using the evidence available I have come to a conclusion which might point to a definitive character for the Arthur which I will now explain.

If we can place our Arthur at the city of Wroxeter as his headquarters then we place him in the ancient kingdom of Powys. It has been suggested that Vortigern was also king of Powys, this would place him ideally for many of the events that surround this period. The fact is there could possibly be two people known as

Vortigern, one the man himself and one actually Vortimer his successor who became assimilated with Vortigern has also been muted and, owing to some of the time periods this could also be likely. Whereas the documentary evidence is not manifold for this period and region we do have other sources. One of the most important being the Pillar of Eliseg which is situated at Vale Crucis (Where St. Collum had his abbey from our story on St. Etheldreda). The pillar claims to be carved with the lineage of Eliseg and even though now it is totally worn away during the 17th century the historian Edward Lhuyd was able to still decipher it and wrote it down for posterity, for which I know history will be eternally grateful. The pillar read as follows:

'Concenn son of Cattell, Cattell son of Brohcmail, Brohcmail son of Eliseg, Eliseg son of Guollauc. Concenn who is therefore great-grandson of Eliseg, erected this stone to his great-grandfather Eliseg. Eliseg annexed the inheritance of Powys...throughout nine years from the power of the English, which he made into a sword land by fire: whosoever shall read this hand inscribed stone, let him give a blessing on the soul of Eliseg: it is Concenn who...with his hand... to his own kingdom of Powys...and which...the mountain...the monarchy Maximus... of Britain... Concenn, Pascent...Maun, Annan: Britu was the son of Vortigern whom Germanus blessed and whom Severa bore to him the daughter of Maximus, the king, who killed the king of the Romans."

The slight problem here is that if we date the evidence we think we know then Vortigern might be little too early for some of the events ascribed to him. We have a hint that Vortimer who was a member of Vortigern's family actually seized control upon Vortigern's death which, we believe might have been down to a natural disaster, as Nennius tells us that divine providence laid him low with hatred for bringing in the Saxon. It is indeed possible that Vortimer may have fought some of the actions ascribed to Vortimer at this time. It is also highly likely that Vortimer could be one and the same as Britu, baptized by St. Germanus.

Whatever the fact behind this we have a date of 459 for Ambrosius, the great Romano Celt leader making a bid for power then. To give him his full name Ambrosius Aurelianus. We are told that his parents' both wore purple' which makes him of high Roman descent. In fact we are told his father was a Roman Consul. He was also an arch enemy of the Vortigern family owing to the disaster of the Saxon furore and numerous treacherous acts against his own family who were still imperialist by sympathy. When the very last legions departed back in 410 AD we are told that Emperor Honorious appointed a 'Comes Britanniarum' or Count of Britain to keep an eye on things for the last vestiges of empire. It is possible that this Comes Britanniarum might have been Ambrosius father. However in 419 we are told that the last Romans were overthrown by the 'Nationalist' Celts and the 'Comes' was withdrawn, but

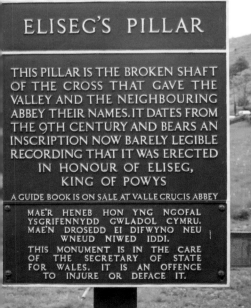

ELISEG'S PILLAR

THIS PILLAR IS THE BROKEN SHAFT OF THE CROSS THAT GAVE THE VALLEY AND THE NEIGHBOURING ABBEY THEIR NAMES. IT DATES FROM THE 9TH CENTURY AND BEARS AN INSCRIPTION NOW BARELY LEGIBLE RECORDING THAT IT WAS ERECTED IN HONOUR OF ELISEG, KING OF POWYS

A GUIDE BOOK IS ON SALE AT VALLE CRUCIS ABBEY

MAE'R HENEB HON YNG NGOFAL YSGRIFENNYDD GWLADOL CYMRU. MAE'N DROSEDD EI DIFWYNO NEU WNEUD NIWED IDDI.

THIS MONUMENT IS IN THE CARE OF THE SECRETARY OF STATE FOR WALES. IT IS AN OFFENCE TO INJURE OR DEFACE IT.

remember there were also 'Imperialist' Romano Celts still in Britain. The Comes son Ambrosius found refuge, we believe in Brittany and there gathered loyal supporters to him to strike back when ready against the Vortigern forces. By the mid 450's Ambrosius was once again in Britain and had by this time gained the south west of Britain and Wales. For a while it appears that Roman imperialism was briefly reintroduced as during the reign of Emperor Anthemius in 470 we are told of British troops fighting for Rome. There has been archaeological proof of a senior British chief residing at Gwynedd during the late 5th century and this could have been the base chosen by Ambrosius.

During this period it is mentioned that the Votadini, the other tribe from the north, came and settled in North West Wales, here again were good troops with which to counter any Saxon incursion. Two of their senior leaders are mentioned as Cunedda and Maglocunus who are also named by Gildas in his work. It would seem that Magloconus soon entrenched himself and his people in Gwynedd and Cunedda and Cuneglasus were ensconced into neighbouring Powys after the demise of Ambrosius thus ensuring that the ancient family of Cunedda, from whom Cuneglasus and Magloconus came, had a seat of power according to their status.

Shortly after this we are informed by the Welsh Genealogies that he is succeeded by Gereuerth who takes over the mantle of King with his capital at Wroxeter. This places him there full square during the campaigns against the Saxons and leader of the Votadini war bands with cavalry from the Alani. The other point of interest is that he married a young lady called Aranwen, daughter of St. Brychan and sister of St. Nectan. Was Nectan, our Cornish saint the brother in law of the man who would become known as the Arthur? Or, indeed, possibly one of the three Arthur candidates? As far as dates and geographical location is concerned it has as much viability as any other theory. I put it forward as a proposition. Then to top it off, just when you thought Brychan's family could not get any more interesting, Nectan's other sister Meleri marries a man called Keredic, their son was called Sant and his son was St. David of Wales! With Nectan as Great Uncle. This would also give us a link with the legend we saw earlier when we saw that King Arthur's knights would visit St. Nectan for vigil and blessing before setting out on a quest or before a great battle. A small kernel of fact in the nut of legend?

## To Summarize:

Rome ruled Britain as part of a great empire. *Fact.*

It appointed district governors with an overall commander to govern. *Fact.*

When Rome retired it left Romano Celts behind. *Fact.*

The old kingdoms started to fight between themselves for power. *Fact.*

Vortigern seized power as High King. *Fact.*

Saxon mercenaries were invited in to assist him. *Fact.*

He forestalled on paying them. *Probability.*

The Saxons started to encroach and take land. *Fact.*

Wales and the south west became the centre for Saxon resistance. *Fact.*

A warlord/king commanded shock troops to hold the Saxons back. *Fact.*

This man was known as the Arthur. *Probability.*

Battles were fought that halted the Saxon advance for forty years. *Fact.*

A mass migration to Brittany took place. *Fact.*

St. David of Wales was Nectan's great-nephew. *Probability.*

Gereuerth of Powys was the Arthur. *Possibility.*

# The Sanctity of Nectan's Glen and Waterfall.

In this final section I want to try and explain why the sacred pool and waterfall that lies at St. Nectan's Glen is still so very powerful in it's spiritual nature for both Christian and Pagan pilgrims. To do this we will look at the Kieve of Nectan and, of course, other sites to observe how sacred water was seen by past cultures and how they still have an effect on us to this day, perhaps even more than ever before.

First let us look at water. Why should it have the effect it does on so many?

Possibly we can answer by describing water as the 'mysterious medium'. By its very substance it changes our perception of things. Water can be calm, still, roaring, fierce, soothing, cooling and life giving all at the same time. It is the one thing (apart from oxygen) that we all need to live. Any culture without water will not survive, so much so that it has taken on a mystical significance for millennia.

Every society has known the importance of water since the world's inception and the dawn of man, it has been described as the blood circulation of the earth and that is just about right. Our early progenitors were renowned for their ability to 'see' water when none was obvious, they would know where to dig for this life force and settlements would grow around those places. A river was by its very nature an obvious supply, a pool the same but some of these locators of early ancestors would divine the sources of underground streams. It is not by accident that all of the ancient stone sites are built over areas of immense underground water activity. These streams and whirlpools, though not seen to the eye, would and do give off radiations of power that were easily divinable to the ancient locators and on these sacred spots the stones were erected and the temples born.

This phenomena was such that as the later faiths overlapped on the earlier ones the sites remained in their condition throughout. Where the great churches and cathedrals now stand, at one time the holy places of the old faiths, they are crisscrossed under their structure with underground water features and pools which have been mapped and doused to confirm their patterns. A number of books have been written on this subject, please look in the bibliography for more information.

In the areas where water was apparent it was easy to understand its importance.

If we look at the realm of ancient Egypt we can see that this mighty nation, one of the most powerful in the ancient world was totally dependent on one thing, the Nile. If the Nile failed, which it had been known to do, Egypt failed. No crops would grow, the granaries would be empty, the people would starve. Egypt looked to the source of the Nile, the blue and the white, and would look for signs of the annual flooding. A natural phenomena takes place when the Nile floods, a few weeks prior to the event the ibis birds flock from the source into Egypt itself and the people would take this as a sign of the flood arriving and ensuring plenteous crops and a fine harvest. The ancient deity of Thoth, the ibis headed god, reflects how important this was. The coming of the ibis was heralded by the priests in the temples as 'Bringer of fortune to the widow, bringer of life to the orphan'.

The Egyptian panoply of gods was immense but each of them were known to all the people, they were the creatures and occurrences they saw each day, they were a divine window into how and why their world worked and flourished or failed. Interestingly when we look at a map of Egypt we see it from the north downwards, not so the Egyptian, they would look at the country from the sources of the Nile hence 'Upper' kingdom Egypt was in the south and 'Lower' kingdom in the north.

In areas where water is not as apparent, such as in Australia or some of

*A painting of St Nectans Kieve by Daniel Maclise 1806-1870, Charles Dickens' sister-in-law, Georgina Hogarth were all regular visitors of St Nectans Kieve. Painting now resides in the Victoria & Albert Museum*

the water is not only cleansing it is the fluid of our birth. It is truly a total and complete re-birth in every sense. When we attended these rituals in our ancient past, or even in pagan rituals today, the pools are the fluid of the Earth Mother herself who gave birth to all the planet over the years and the pools can be seen as the womb of the sacred Mother. I mentioned earlier the Chalice Well pool at Glastonbury, this is so evident there you can feel it flow through your very soul.

I am always reminded of a saying by dear old Mark Twain (Sam Clemens), who remarked "I was dead for millions of years before I was born and it didn't bother me in the slightest". A super comment and one we can adapt to view this whole subject of rebirth. If we take in to account previous existences, if you believe in that possibility, then a rebirth would be an unlocking of a great door with astonishing potential results.

Because of the importance of the sacred pools and streams that give us this cleansing, this chance to be born again literally a new lease of life, it is only natural for the water to mean even more to those who look upon it as a tool, a sacred article if you will with which to practice their religious and spiritual paths. One of the most common of these has been scrying, a means whereby the practitioner gazes into a pool or bowl of still water and thereby becomes part of the living depths. Many believe that visions can be obtained by this practice (Dr John Dee used both this method and also the use of a 'scrying disc' of polished obsidian) in which to concentrate the gaze. However, it is normally seen as the practice of "Know thyself" that here comes into play.

The discovery of the self without which any further ritual work is pointless.

We must recognize the potential of subjective self awareness as being vital for our spiritual cleansing prior to any sacred journey or quest. It was not a coincidence that in the grail legends our hero Galahad, or Percival depending on the version you read, loses everything before the grail is attained. During the quest he recognizes his own frailty and misgivings with results that would at seem at first glance to be self destructive but after the realization of the 'faults' and the knowledge of their destructive nature to his divine essence then, when all seems lost, he achieves the grail and only then.

The cleansing nature of the waters has been recognized for aeons and the very nature of undergoing a purification ritual is to surrender yourself to a greater will and awareness. Some may feel that a baptismal cleansing and rebirth might be a palliative effect but let's bear in mind that at times it is the effect of the so-called palliative that allows the divine spark to be released, the supra is, that indefinable something receives recognition from the knowledge that, placebo or not, it is being seen to exist and therefore flourishes.

If we therefore look at the pools, springs and waters that may appear to us as spiritually renewing then it is not just enough to allow the waters to 'do their thing'. Any form of spiritual exercise must by its very nature be interactive.

Even with main stream faiths it is not acceptable to be a participant and not react with the ritual in which you participate. Blind and unthinking ritual when learned by rote or just witnessed as a matter of form has no beneficial effect on the individual. Indeed, the Hebrew faith actively encourages questioning as a useful form of re-energizing the belief in the faith and it works very well!

If we allow ourselves the ability to work spiritually with the waters, to let ourselves be cleansed and to gaze down into the depths or through the rapid currents of the falls, it is easy to see one more aspect of the waters blessings that are given to us. Water, as a medium that is both known and alien to us, can be perceived by us as with our distant ancestors, as an entry way or

portal into another world. A world where we can go and yet cannot survive.

Where we can glimpse but cannot stay. It simply cries out to us the Celtic belief in the 'Other' worlds, those existences that coincide with ours, the very dawn of the multiverse theories and yet known and believed by our forebears two thousand years ago.

Interaction then is vital. So, how do we interact with the element of water?

To our ancestors it was simple, you gave offerings and thanks. It is refreshing to witness that now, in our scientific world, more and more people are being seen to not just take for granted the gift of water and/or the use of its cleansing and ritual properties. Ritual offerings to pools and perhaps their attendant deities has been seen as 'doing our part' since our belief systems began. Many still exist and in such ways that those taking part might not even be aware any longer why they are doing what they do. In Estonia it was long the custom for the people of a village to takes boats out onto their rivers and pools and once there they would strew flowers onto the waters surface, thus ensuring the continuing plentiful supply of the sweet, fresh water. An interesting fact is that each year at Eton College, near Windsor (otherwise known as Slough Grammar) the boys decorate their straw boater hats with garlands of flowers and then take punts out onto the River Thames and when out they remove their hats and shake the flowers intothe waters thus giving offerings to the Goddess Flora.

In earlier times offerings of a more substantial nature would be made, in particular I am reminded of the magnificent bronze shield that was uncovered from the Thames near Battersea, now bearing its name, and the wonder its discovery caused. An offering, if it is to made at all, should not just be a token offering, it should be something special that has feeling and thought behind it. For those who attend a parish church and each week place a few coins into the offertory it may mean nothing, but for some, when that offering is more than they can afford then that offering is made with heart-felt sincerity. So it was with our ancestors, shield, spears, swords, bowls, all of these offerings were made with sincerity and many were of great intrinsic value.

We can see echoes of this with the legend of the Lady in the Lake. How would it be if I told you she was real? Each pool, spring, lake had its attendant priestess; it was she who supervised the offerings made. After the death of a great warlord it would be quite normal for an intimate article of his be given as an offering to the local sacred waters and it would also be in order that, after a short passage of time, his successor could approach the priestess and the sword would be drawn back out of the pool by her and presented to him as a re-energized item. Itself it has been cleansed and purified by the action of being in the scared waters. This is very possibly the origin of the presenting of the sword Excalibur to the Arthur.

It is for this reason that many people make offerings to the sacred pools, as at St. Nectan's, by leaving something in its waters to be either a votive to the Goddess or to be placed there temporarily in order to re-energize the offering giving it the rebirth and renewal that the same waters offer to us. It is very evident when visiting St. Nectan's Kieve how importantly this ritual is taken by many people. As we mentioned earlier Nectan was one of the early Celtic brotherhood, his whole reason for being was to evangelize the new faith in his way, which was not encumbered by a hierarchy situated across Europe.

His faith worked with the old beliefs and he would have taught not by forceful transplanting a dogma on to an existing belief but by showing the similarity in worship between them. For Goddess Nectan would read Holy Mother, this assimilation worked well with the population, probably why the Celtic church was received with a warm transition in many places. Nectan recognized the importance of the seasons, the ever changing scenes of the land being farmed, the needs of the people and the oneness that existed between the people, the land, the Goddess and him. We mentioned earlier that water was seen as the blood circulation of the world. Every man ,woman and child was aware of its vital part in their everyday survival, living with it and through it and in it. Nectan's Kieve was a place where they could reach out and actually touch the power of the living spirit that flowed throughout their world. By making their offerings and by giving their prayers they had committed to being a part of it, they had achieved that true interactive faith that we have seen is so vital. Many people thought that the world was a part of the spirit of a huge dragon and that the pools and lakes were the dragon's gateway of entry and exit from its world to theirs. The dragon was seen as part of the Goddess, as the dragon was the masculine and fiery element so the Goddess was also there to use his strength and add her calming coolness of the waters to make the two beings one force. Two polar opposites that unite to create the most powerful living force.

It is still the custom for pilgrims of all callings to leave offerings at Nectan's Kieve, sometimes asking for intercession on behalf of a loved one or a project to benefit others, other times simply as offerings of thanks, thanks for the cleansing and healing powers or even thanks for just being.

Nectan's Kieve remains to this day what it always has been, an area of tranquillity and of self realization as well as a place of interaction between ourselves and the great force that guides us. It is all in one, our place for communicating with the Goddess, the Holy Mother, the Dragon and Nectan himself. The sanctity transcends boundaries, the prayers have no walls, the divine is remains present and all will be well.


*Blessed be.*

We first came here by chance on 14th October 2012, the day after our 49th anniversary not knowing what we would find.

The place affected us both. We spent time by the waterfall and found ourselves remembering friends and family who have gone and threw a stone into the river thinking of them.

We returned today with this marker to remember the people who those who helped us over the years; to mark our love for our fam our children and their children; but especially for each other.

One day this will fall into the river and become part of it aga We hope it's left where it falls because that's how it shou

ANITA and FRED - married 12th October 1963
"All you need is love"

St. Nectans Waterfall from above

St. Nectans Waterfall view of the opening

*Second Waterfall at St. Nectans Glen*

# An Index of major names and places from the text.

# Bibliography:

**'Secret Shrines'.**

Paul Broadhurst.

*A first class and well researched book dealing with the Cornish plethora of sacred wells and springs.*

**'The Oxford Dictionary of Saints'.**

David Farmer.

*Expertly researched and a 'must' for any student of the sacred personages of sainthood.*

**'King Arthur. The True Story'.**

Graham Phillips and Martin Keatman.

*Excellent book showing much study into the Welsh genealogies.*

**'Living Christianity'.**

Martin Palmer.

*Magnificent study of Christianity and its place in the world past and present.*

**'The Worlds Most Mysterious Places'.**

Lionel and Patricia Fanthorpe.

*Beautifully written work dealing with a wide range of sacred sites and mystic practices.*

**'History of Britain and Welsh Annals'.**

Nennius.

*A seminal piece of primary source material invaluable to any student.*

**'Of The Ruin Of Britain'.**

Gildas.

*Again a piece of primary source material from a man who lived during the period in question.*

**'The Golden Bough'.**

J. G. Frazer.

*A huge and breathtaking study of the worlds magical practices.*

**'The Age Of Arthur'.**

John Morris.

*A truly spectacular piece of work, one of the first to tackle the history around the legend and still the best.*

**'Fentynyow Kernow'**

Cheryl Straffon.

*Terrific book that should be a staple for any pilgrim of the trail.*

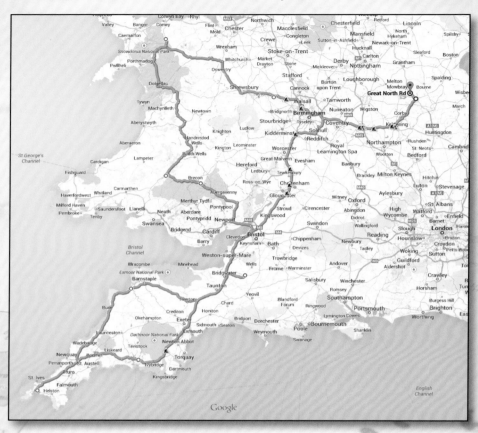

The Challenge: Cover over 1,100 miles, 30 sites, with some amazing and spectacular views and good weather! From The Midlands, North Wales, West Wales, Somerset, Devon and Cornwall and back again.

I met some fantastic, friendly and helpful people on my journey, some sites were not easily accessible but worth it when I got there.

A big thank you to Celia, Molly & Tom as well as everyone that helped, assisted, guided and pointed me in the right direction.

For a more indepth look at the journey, please visit:
**www.st-nectansglen.co.uk/sacred-falls-journey**

## DAY 1 - Sunday

*Wales*

The Wrekin. Shropshire.
Wroxeter. (Roman Town). Shropshire.
Vale Crucis Abbey. Llangollen.
Pillar of Eliseg. Llangollen.

## DAY 2 - Monday

*Wales*

Brecon Beacons.
Brecon Town.

*Somerset*

Glastonbury Abbey.
Spring Head. Chalice Well Gardens.
The White Spring.

## DAY 3 - Tuesday

*Cornwall and West*

St Nectan's Church: Hartland, Stoke, Devon.
St Morwenna's Well. Morwenstow. Cornwall
St John's Church. Morwenstow.
St Neot's Well. Poundstock
Jetwells Well. Camelford.
Davidstow Holy Well. Boscastle.
St Nectan's Glen. Trethevy.
St Piran's. Chapel. Trethevy.
St Piran's Well. Trethevy.
Chapel Well. St Breward.
St Guron's Well. Bodmin.

## DAY 4 - Wednesday

*Cornwall and West*

Holywell Bay, Cornwall
St Winnow's Church. Lostwithiel.
Sancreed Holy Well. Sancreed.
St Pedtr's Well. Treloy.

Cover photo by Don Taylor, Canberra, Australia
Back cover photo by Guy Mills
Photo's and design by Neil Alexander
Additional photo's by Phillip Bramhill LBIPP
Photo of Roland Rotherham on page 3 by Mr David Overend

ISBN: 978-0-9930282-0-5